THE QUEENS OF FASHION:

Linda Evangelista, Christy Turlington, Naomi Campbell, and Cindy Crawford

Linda A. Walker

TABLE OF CONTENT

10:2 Staying Ageless and Stylish

CONCLUSION

INTRODUCTION

In the realm of fashion, some names have an unmistakable resonance that captures a certain age, redefines beauty, and captures the spirit of a generation. They are legends, style icons, and representations of ageless grace in addition to being supermodels. These four women are the fashion industry's queens: Cindy Crawford, Christy Turlington, Naomi Campbell, and Linda Evangelista.

A sea change occurred in the fashion business during the 1990s. Boundaries were stretched, conventions were broken, and four supermodels came to the forefront of the world's attention at that time. Not merely faces on magazine covers or mannequins on the runway, Linda, Christy, Naomi, and Cindy were cultural icons. They stood for a fresh interpretation of beauty, an unreserved self-assurance, and a significant impact that went beyond the runway and permeated the minds of a generation.

In "The Queens of Fashion," we set out to explore the lives and enduring contributions of these four remarkable women who collectively shaped a decade. Every one of them had a distinct charm, extraordinary talent, and a tale that millions of people could relate to. Together, they created an alliance that was as much about ferocious rivalry as it was about friendship, pushing the boundaries of the fashion world and transforming it in the process.

We explore the lives of these extraordinary women as we read through the book's pages, learning about their quick ascent to prominence, their unique contributions to the fashion industry, and their enduring influence on society as a whole. Each chapter reveals a new aspect of their unstoppable presence, from Linda's daring to Christy's grace, Naomi's pioneering energy to Cindy's broad appeal.

Beyond their glitzy exteriors, we also look at their individual and group charitable endeavors, their support of causes close to their hearts, and the lessons they have taught about empowerment and self-belief. These queens have transformed many people's lives and are more than just style icons—they are role models who have gone beyond the catwalk.

In addition to honoring their aesthetic contributions to the world, "The Queens of Fashion" pays tribute to their lasting influence on fashion, beauty, culture, and other fields. It explores a time when four amazing women ruled supreme, enthralling and inspiring the globe and demonstrating the unbounded splendor of beauty.

Come celebrate the queens who continue to brighten our lives with their grace, spirit, and enduring influence as we relive the magic of the 1990s, the decade that gave us Linda, Christy, Naomi, and Cindy.

CHAPTER 1: THE 90'S FASHION REVOLUTION

The foursome of Linda Evangelista, Christy Turlington, Naomi Campbell, and Cindy Crawford personified the fashion revolution of the 1990s. Their combined influence and impact changed the fashion business in several ways, including:

Diversity and Inclusion: In an industry that was frequently chastised for its dearth of representation, these supermodels were instrumental in advancing diversity and inclusion. They defied conventional notions of beauty, opening the door for models from a variety of backgrounds.

Self-reliance and assurance: Their powerful and assured presence in fashion advertisements and on runways inspired others to value their individuality and feel empowered. They served as representations of poise and confidence.

Adaptability and Versatility: They redefined the standards for models with their chameleon-like ability to change their appearances and adapt to various styles. They gained notoriety for taking on many characters.

Fashion Trendsetters: Their impact went beyond modeling as they created fresh looks that are still relevant in today's world of fashion. Their famous photoshoots and ad campaigns became symbols of creativity.

Cultural Icons: These supermodels rose to prominence as globally recognizable cultural icons. Films, music videos, and other popular culture mediums widely included and praised their imagery.

Advocacy and Philanthropy: Following the 1990s, they took advantage of their notoriety to promote vital social causes, such as diversity, children's welfare, and maternal health. Their charitable endeavors illustrated the beneficial influence supermodels might have on the community.

Linda Evangelista, Christy Turlington, Naomi Campbell, and Cindy Crawford led the '90s fashion revolution, which had a significant and long-lasting effect on society standards, the fashion business, and culture. They left an enduring legacy of innovation and change by reshaping the industry's principles, fostering diversity, and enabling people to embrace their individuality.

1:1 The Era of Change and Innovation

These four enduring supermodels had a major influence on the development of the 1990s, which was a decade of innovation and transformation in the fashion industry. Here's how they helped usher in a period of invention and change:

Diversity and Inclusion: In the fashion industry, Linda Evangelista, Christy Turlington, Naomi Campbell, and Cindy Crawford championed diversity and inclusion by questioning conventional notions of beauty. Their participation signaled a change in modeling toward inclusivity and representation.

Versatility and Adaptability: They were incredibly creative in their ability to change into many looks and poses. They demonstrated that models could be successful in a variety of fashion genres, setting a new benchmark for adaptability.

Individuality and Empowerment: These supermodels represented empowerment and individuality in addition to being just pretty faces. They exhorted individuals to value their individuality and to feel comfortable in their flesh.

Trendsetters: They created new fashion trends that are still relevant today, therefore their influence went beyond the catwalk. Their memorable moments from fashion advertisements and photography come to represent innovation.

Advocacy and Philanthropy: After the 1990s, they utilized their notoriety to support worthy causes, such as diversity, maternal health, and the welfare of young people. Their charitable endeavors were avant-garde in that they illustrated the beneficial effects supermodels could have on society.

Cultural Icons: They had an impact outside of the fashion sector. They rose to prominence as global cultural icons and were regularly showcased in movies and music videos, among other media.

An era of innovation and reinvention was ushered in by Christy Turlington, Linda Evangelista, Cindy Crawford, and Naomi Campbell. They defied industry conventions, supported significant social causes, and had a lasting impression on fashion and society, proving the ability of supermodels to change the world in which they live.

1:2 The Rise of the Supermodels

These four enduring personalities were crucial in redefining the term "supermodel" during the transformative 1990s period in fashion history. The supermodels rose to prominence as a result of their combined influence and presence:

International Recognition: Despite boundaries and linguistic barriers, Linda Evangelista, Christy Turlington, Naomi Campbell, and Cindy Crawford became faces that were known throughout the world.

Revolutionized Beauty Standards: By exhibiting a variety of looks, stressing the value of embracing individuality, and shattering barriers that had previously restricted the industry's inclusivity, these supermodels together revolutionized traditional beauty standards.

Self-reliance and assurance: Their commanding and self-assured appearance in fashion advertisements and on the runways was inspiring. They demonstrated that a supermodel may represent empowerment and confidence in addition to being a model.

Versatility: They were revolutionary in their ability to change up their looks and styles throughout a single photo session. It demonstrated their adaptability, which reflected the fashion industry's energy.

Trendsetters: They had a significant impact on fashion trends as well, redefining what was possible for models to do and establishing new benchmarks for style. Even now, people still remember their legendary moments from advertisements and the runway.

Advocacy for Change: All of them have utilized their notoriety to promote important social and health issues in addition to fashion, proving that supermodels can be powerful advocates for change.

In the fashion world, the ascent of Cindy Crawford, Christy Turlington, Naomi Campbell, and Linda

Evangelista represented a turning point. These were more than simply supermodels; they were cultural icons who pushed for originality, reinterpreted what it meant to be beautiful, and established new benchmarks for empowerment and adaptability. Their enduring legacy is still influencing the modeling industry and the fashion world.

CHAPTER 2: LINDA EVANGELISTA: THE CHAMELEON

In the world of fashion, Linda Evangelista is known for her adaptability and plasticity. She rightfully got the nickname "The Chameleon" for her amazing ability to change and modify her appearance. Linda was born in St. Catharines, Ontario, Canada, on May 10, 1965. Her entry into the modeling industry turned out to be remarkable.

The late 1980s and early 1990s, sometimes known as the "era of the supermodel," are credited with her ascent to stardom. Evangelista was essential in influencing the fashion scene of that era, as were other models like Christy Turlington, Cindy Crawford, and Naomi Campbell. Linda was distinguished by her remarkable features as well as her extraordinary adaptability.

Linda Evangelista was unique in that she was open to accepting change. She was renowned for her constantly changing hairstyles and hues, which encouraged many ladies to play around with their appearances. Her well-known statement, "We don't wake up for less than $10,000 a day," has endured as a representation of the opulence and elegance of the supermodel era.

Throughout her career, Linda Evangelista appeared on the covers of prominent fashion publications, walked the runways for well-known designers, and starred in several commercials. Her partnerships with designers like Karl Lagerfeld and photographers like Steven Meisel produced timeless fashion moments that are still cherished today.

Evangelista's professionalism and devotion to her craft, together with her ability to modify her style, made her a popular figure in the fashion business. For many years, she dominated the international fashion industry by constantly reinventing herself and influencing upcoming models.

Although Linda Evangelista's extensive career as a model has left a lasting impression, her influence goes beyond the world of fashion. She started advocating for breast cancer awareness, stressing the value of research and early detection. Another aspect of her chameleon-like nature is her ability to switch between multiple positions, such as spokesman and model.

As a living example of the strength of adaptation and reinvention, Linda Evangelista is still regarded as a legendary personality in the fashion industry. Her reputation as "The Chameleon" has left a lasting impression on the dynamic world of fashion, where change is not only welcomed but also applauded.

2:1 A Supermodel of Versatility

As a supermodel with extraordinary range, Linda
Evangelista has well-earned her reputation. Her career
has been distinguished by her capacity to change, grow,
and succeed in a variety of fashion-related fields. She is
hailed as a versatile supermodel for the following
reasons:

The Chameleon: Because of her amazing ability to
change into different personas for photo shoots and
runway shows, Evangelista is frequently referred to as
"The Chameleon". She created a new benchmark for
modeling versatility with her ability to adopt a variety of
personas and styles.

Varieties of Collaborations: She has collaborated with a
wide range of stylists, photographers, and designers,
demonstrating her versatility in moving between high
fashion and commercial modeling. Her flexibility is

demonstrated by her partnerships with some of the most prominent names in the industry.

Fashion Icon: Evangelista's sense of style and memorable runway moments have had a long-lasting influence on the fashion industry. She has become a true fashion legend due to her impact on style trends and her capacity to establish new benchmarks for the industry.

Enduring Beauty: Throughout her career, she has maintained her demand due to her timeless beauty and classic characteristics. Her ongoing popularity is demonstrated by her ability to keep up a fascinating presence both in front of the camera and on the runway.

Activist for Maternal Health: In addition to her career in fashion, Linda Evangelista has devoted her time to advocating for maternal health. Her efforts have demonstrated her adaptability in harnessing her celebrity for a worthwhile cause by bringing attention to the pressing problems of maternal mortality and the significance of safe childbirth.

Legacy of Influence: Models, designers, and the fashion industry at large are all still motivated by her legendary moments and capacity for transformation. Because of her ongoing influence, Linda Evangelista is still regarded as a supermodel with incredible flexibility and effect.

2:2 Iconic Moments and Transformations

In the modeling industry, Linda Evangelista has left a history of memorable events and revolutions. The following are a few of her career's pivotal moments that have cemented her place as an icon:

The Chameleon: Linda Evangelista's extraordinary ability to change appearances for the camera and the runway led to her being dubbed "The Chameleon". She was able to exhibit her breadth and flexibility by taking on many characters and styles because of her versatility.

Short Hair Revolution: Her renowned short haircut in the early 1990s is among her most recognizable moments. This audacious move transformed the fashion and beauty industries, creating a worldwide trend and raising the bar for hairstyles.

Visibility in Fashion: Evangelista's adaptability made her a highly sought-after model in the business, enabling her to collaborate with a wide range of stylists, designers, and photographers. She established a benchmark for versatility and success across a range of fashion categories.

Timeless Beauty: Linda Evangelista has been in demand for decades due to her timeless beauty. She is a representation of timeless grace and beauty due to her timeless features, compelling presence, and beautiful eyes.

Maternal Health Advocacy: Evangelista has devoted her time to maternal health advocacy after leaving the modeling industry. She has used her notoriety to spread the word about the significance of safe childbirth and maternal mortality.

Enduring Influence: Her enduring influence is highlighted by the fact that her memorable historical events still serve as an inspiration to modern fashion designers and models.

Linda Evangelista's career has been distinguished by her ability to shift on the runway, her daring haircut choices, her adaptability in the fashion world, and her commitment to significant causes. She is still a timeless icon whose impact is still felt in the fashion industry.

CHAPTER 3: CHRISTY TURLINGTON: TIMELESS GRACE

Within the realm of fashion and modeling, some names endure and come to represent timeless grace and beauty. Among these icons is Christy Turlington, who is frequently referred to as a representation of "Timeless Grace." Not only has her remarkable career lasted decades, but it has also left a lasting impression on the industry and beyond.

Christy Turlington was born in Walnut Creek, California, on January 2, 1969, and her career as a model started at a young age. Her composure and grace immediately made her stand out, indicating that greatness was in her future. Her inner grace and dignity are reflected in her beauty, which transcends beyond appearances.

Christy Turlington stands out for her ability to go above the ever-evolving fashion trends. She is more than just a model; she is the epitome of classic beauty. Her timeless elegance and sophistication make her appealing even in the face of the fashion industry's continuous change.

Turlington has been the inspiration for some of the most renowned designers and photographers in the world during her lengthy career. Numerous classic moments, including magazine covers and runways at the most prominent fashion events, have been produced by her collaborations.

However, Christy Turlington's influence goes beyond the fashion industry. She has shown her versatility by pursuing endeavors in acting and lobbying, among other fields. Her commitment to changing the world for the better is evident in her work as an advocate for maternal health.

Christy Turlington, a representation of "Timeless Grace," has not only remained relevant but also expanded upon it throughout time. Her grace and elegance are a constant source of inspiration and influence in the fashion industry, serving as a reminder that grace and beauty are timeless and unaffected by fads or fashion.

Christy Turlington's everlasting presence serves as a reminder of the staying power of beauty and sophistication in an industry that is known for continual change. For many more decades to come, her reputation as a timeless icon in the fashion and charitable worlds will be radiant. Christy Turlington is a living example of "Timeless Grace" in a society that is constantly looking for the newest, biggest thing.

3:1 The Epitome of Elegance

In the modeling business, Christy Turlington is regarded by many as the height of elegance. In the world of fashion, her composure, grace, and ageless beauty have elevated her to the status of a refined Epitome of Elegance. She is praised for her grace for the following reasons:

Timeless Beauty: Turlington's beauty is ageless and stands the test of time, regardless of fashion. Throughout her career, her timeless features and subtle elegance have continued to captivate.

Simplicity in Fashion: Christy frequently wears sophisticated yet understated looks. Her style is evident in the way she can turn even the most basic dress into something effortlessly exquisite.

Grace on the Runway: She stands out from the crowd with an unmatched grace when she walks the runway. She radiates a sophisticated refinement and wears expensive clothes with ease.

Advocacy and Philanthropy: Turlington's devotion to philanthropy and advocacy for maternal health highlights her determination to have a positive social influence, highlighting her grace in both appearance and personality.

Iconic picture: Her picture is still honored and cited in a variety of media, demonstrating her lasting impact as a symbol of grace and beauty.

Christy Turlington is praised for her classic beauty, understated sense of style, poise on the catwalk, charitable endeavors, and legendary stature. She truly is the pinnacle of elegance, and her continuing popularity is proof of her ageless beauty.

3:2 Impact Beyond the Catwalk

Christy Turlington has a major influence in many different fields, and her reach goes well beyond the catwalk. Here's a closer look at her influence outside of the modeling industry:

Maternal Health Advocate: Outside of modeling, Turlington is most known for her support of maternal health. As the creator of "Every Mother Counts," she has improved access to safe childbirth and increased awareness of maternal mortality by using her notoriety. Her work has significantly impacted the healthcare industry and saved lives.

Documentary Filmmaker: Turlington has dabbled in the field of documentaries, producing films that highlight important social and medical concerns. Her documentaries have sparked constructive change in addition to increasing awareness.

Philanthropy: Her commitment to improving society is demonstrated by her support of charitable projects, especially those related to maternal health. Numerous people throughout the world have been impacted by her charitable activity.

Cultural Influence: Turlington's image endures as a timeless representation of grace, elegance, and beauty, even beyond the scope of her advocacy activities. Her cultural impact can be seen in pop culture and a variety of media.

Inspiration for Aspiring Models: Aspiring models can draw inspiration from Turlington's path from the runway to her influential advocacy activities. She shows how achieving success in the field can serve as a springboard for making significant contributions to society.

The influence Christy Turlington has outside of the catwalk highlights the tremendous potential of leveraging celebrity for good. Her commitment to philanthropy, documentary filmmaking, and maternal health advocacy has had a significant impact and is an incredible example of how a supermodel can be a force for good in the world.

CHAPTER 4: NAOMI CAMBELL: THE CATWALK QUEEN

Few names in the fashion industry are as well-known as Naomi Campbell's. Known as "The Catwalk Queen," she is a legendary supermodel whose impact has spanned multiple generations. Her place as a true fashion legend has been cemented by her incredible career and long-lasting influence on the industry.

Naomi Campbell was born in London, England, on May 22, 1970, and her career as a model started early. She was discovered when she was fifteen years old, and in the late eighties, she became one of the most sought-after models of her time.

Naomi Campbell has earned her reputation as "The Catwalk Queen" as she has walked innumerable runways across the globe and made a lasting impression with her enticing walk and powerful presence. She stood out from the crowd on the runway because of her ability to change like a chameleon and effortlessly fit into the ideas of different designers.

Her effort in dismantling racial boundaries is among her most notable achievements in the fashion business. As one of the first black models to become a global celebrity, Naomi utilized her platform to promote inclusivity and diversity in the fashion industry. She cleared the path for upcoming generations of diverse model talent.

In addition to her talent on the runway, Naomi was featured on the covers of some of the most prominent fashion magazines in the world. Her partnerships with famous photographers and designers resulted in timeless fashion moments that are still cherished today. Her visage came to represent the pinnacle of elegance and beauty.

In addition to her acting career, Campbell has pursued business endeavors, showcasing her adaptability and spirit of entrepreneurship. Her talent and personality have been shown off outside of the runway with appearances in movies and TV series.

Naomi Campbell has encountered difficulties and controversy along the way, but her fortitude and tenacity have only enhanced her legendary reputation. She is still a major force behind industry reform and a global impact in the fashion world.

"The Catwalk Queen" is more than just a moniker; it's evidence of Naomi Campbell's continuing influence on the fashion industry. She will always be remembered as a representation of the strength and beauty found in the modeling industry because of her walk, her presence, and her unshakable dedication to diversity. As the fashion industry continues to change, Naomi Campbell is still a source of inspiration for aspiring models and a representation of advancement.

4:1 A Trailblazer in the Industry

In the fashion world, Naomi Campbell is without a doubt a trailblazer who paved the way for change and left a lasting impression. The following are some of the main factors that have made her a trailblazer:

Diversity Advocate: Naomi Campbell has tirelessly pushed for inclusion and diversity in the fashion industry. She advocated for models from a variety of racial and ethnic origins, challenging the underrepresentation in the industry.

Iconic Runway Presence: She created a new benchmark with her dominant runway presence. With her striking catwalk performances, she broke new ground and redefined what it meant to be the owner of the runway.

Bold and daring Fashion Decisions: Naomi broke conventions and established new benchmarks for honesty and self-assurance in modeling with her audacious and daring attitude to fashion.

Longevity and Relevance: She has a career that surpasses expectations in the sector. She is still in demand and important today, proving that a model can make a lasting difference in a field that is always changing.

Global Icon: Naomi Campbell is not just a model; her impact goes well beyond that. She is revered and known all over the world, in all countries and civilizations.

Activism and Advocacy: She demonstrated that models can be powerful voices for change by using her notoriety to promote significant social causes. Her charitable endeavors have had a noteworthy influence.

Pioneering Spirit: Naomi broke down barriers and demonstrated that the fashion industry could become more inclusive by paving the way for upcoming generations of models.

Through her groundbreaking career, which has redefined the fashion business, Naomi Campbell has shown the world what it means to be bold and real, showcased stunning runway performances, and advocated for diversity and inclusivity. She is still a major player in the fashion industry and an inspiration to people who want to change the face of the business.

4.2 Defying Expectations and Setting Standards

Supermodel Naomi Campbell is known for continuously shattering expectations and establishing new benchmarks in the fashion business. The following significant facets of her career demonstrate her capacity to defy expectations and set new standards:

Promoter of Diversity: In the fashion industry, Naomi Campbell has been a steadfast supporter of inclusiveness and diversity. Through her advocacy for increased inclusion of models from a variety of racial and cultural origins, she has confronted the systematic inequalities in the business and established new benchmarks.

Fearless Fashion Choices: She has distinguished herself with her daring and fearless sense of style. In the modeling industry, Naomi has set the bar for confidence and genuineness by being unashamedly herself.

Iconic Catwalk Presence: She has raised the bar for runway performance with her strong and authoritative presence on the catwalk. She has a legendary ability to attract crowds and own the runway.

Longevity in the Industry: Naomi's long career contradicts the perception of modeling success as a transitory state. In a field that is renowned for its rapid change, she has established a benchmark for durability and significance.

Advocacy for Social Causes: Naomi has shown that models can be powerful advocates for change by utilizing her notoriety and influence to promote significant social causes in addition to fashion.

Cultural Icon: Naomi Campbell is a cultural icon in addition to being a supermodel. Her reputation and impact are well-known and appreciated outside of the fashion industry.

the career of Naomi Campbell has been distinguished by her dedication to diversity, her audacious fashion choices, her legendary catwalk presence, her longevity, her advocacy, and her position as a cultural icon. She has challenged the fashion industry to be more real and inclusive by setting new standards and defying expectations.

CHAPTER 5: CINDY CRAWFORD: THE ALL- AMERICAN ICON

In the realms of fashion and entertainment, Cindy Crawford's name has come to represent "The All-American Icon". She was born in DeKalb, Illinois, on February 20, 1966. She became well-known in the late 1980s and early 1990s and her influence has lasted ever since.

Cindy Crawford is "The All-American Icon" because she embodies traditional American beauty. She won the hearts and minds of viewers everywhere with her gorgeous beauty, signature mole, and innate charm. She is a cherished figure in the industry because of her appeal across generations and cultural boundaries.

Cindy Crawford's career has been distinguished by her extensive modeling gigs. She became a sought-after subject for leading designers and photographers, appearing on the covers of most esteemed fashion journals. Her partnerships with industry titans like Herb Ritts and Richard Avedon resulted in some of the most recognizable fashion photos of her time.

Cindy's influence goes beyond her time as a model. She is renowned for her business ventures as well, having started a lucrative line of home furnishings and cosmetics. Her adaptability and business sense are demonstrated by her ability to go from modeling to the corporate world.

Her status as "The All-American Icon" has also had an impact on the entertainment industry. She leaped into acting, appearing in movies, TV series, and music videos, proving she could broaden her skill set and increase her audience.

Cindy Crawford has also shown her dedication to having a beneficial influence on society by using her position to promote several charity projects. Her charitable endeavors reveal the complexity of her personality and the principles that have sustained her legendary reputation.

In the worlds of fashion and entertainment, Cindy Crawford is a timeless symbol due to her ongoing appeal and representation of American beauty and ideals. She has established a benchmark for grace, elegance, and adaptability, serving as a constant reminder that genuine icons are those who enthrall and inspire people of all ages.

"The All-American Icon" is more than simply a title—it's an endorsement of Cindy Crawford's influence on the entertainment, fashion, and charitable industries. For years to come, her legacy will remain a shining example of traditional American beauty and a lasting impact.

5:1 A Supermodel with Global Appeal

Cindy Crawford is without a doubt a supermodel with a broad following. She has become a household name not just in the world of fashion but also across national boundaries due to her legendary status and impact. Cindy Crawford is known as a supermodel with global appeal for the following main reasons:

Timeless Beauty: Everyone is in awe of Cindy Crawford's beauty. People of many origins and civilizations have been drawn to her timeless beauty and inherent charm.

Versatility: She is a relatable and versatile character in the fashion industry due to her ability to adjust to many aesthetics and fashion styles. She can transition between elegant and more casual outfits with ease, making her appealing to a wide range of consumers.

Cultural Icon: From her appearances in music videos to her position as a worldwide brand ambassador, Cindy Crawford's image and impact are ubiquitous in popular culture. Her influence on culture has made her a globally recognizable and approachable figure.

Advocacy: Her commitment to child welfare and philanthropy is evidence of her international influence. People who value her dedication to having a good global effect find resonance in her advocacy work.

Enduring Legacy: Her appeal is timeless and universal due to her extended tenure in the fashion industry and her ongoing significance.

Cindy Crawford's timeless beauty, adaptability, cultural relevance, advocacy, and capacity for global human connection are all factors in her appeal. She epitomizes everything that makes a supermodel, her impact boundless.

5:2 Enduring Influence and Style

"Cindy Crawford's enduring influence and style are a testament to her iconic stature in the world of fashion and beauty. Here are some significant features of her continuing influence and style:

Timeless Beauty: Cindy Crawford's beauty has endured the test of time. Her classic features, especially her signature mole, have made her a symbol of enduring and natural beauty.

Wardrobe Icon: Crawford's wardrobe choices have always mixed traditional elegance with comfort. Her style is characterized by a mix of classic pieces that stress both style and comfort, setting her apart as a fashion star.

Versatility: Her ability to adapt to several fashion trends, from high fashion to casual clothing, displays her versatility and guarantees that her impact remains current.

Entrepreneurship: Crawford's endeavors into entrepreneurship, especially her lucrative beauty product lines and furniture collections, highlight her versatility and her capability to flourish in numerous industries.

Philanthropy: She is an advocate for children's welfare and actively supports children's hospitals and philanthropic projects aimed at improving the lives of children, showcasing her passion for creating a beneficial influence beyond fashion.

Cultural Icon: Cindy Crawford's enduring influence extends into popular culture, as her image continues to be recognized and praised in various forms of media, from music videos to film appearances.

Cindy Crawford's enduring influence and style may be summed up as a blend of timeless beauty, adaptability, enterprise, philanthropy, and cultural icon status. She remains a symbol of elegance and grace, both in the fashion world and in society at large.

CHAPTER 6: COLLECTIVE POWER: THE SUPERMODEL SQUAD

Known as the "Supermodel Squad," Linda Evangelista, Christy Turlington, Naomi Campbell, and Cindy Crawford represented a group force that changed the fashion business and had an impact that went beyond the catwalk. Their partnership and shared experiences had an unforgettable influence on the world of fashion. Here's a closer look at their collective power:

Redefining Beauty Standards: As a group, they challenged established beauty standards and championed diversity in the industry. Their presence marked a move towards a more inclusive and representative image of beauty.

flexibility and Adaptability: Their ability to alter and adapt to many styles demonstrated their flexibility, challenging the assumption that models had to fit into a set mold. They emphasized that flexibility and adaptability were crucial in the ever-evolving fashion business.

Fashion Influence: The Supermodel Squad set several fashion trends, inspiring designers, photographers, and fashion fans alike. Their spectacular moments on runways and in ads left a lasting mark on the industry.

Cultural Icons: They transcended the fashion business to become cultural icons, renowned and admired beyond the bounds of their profession. Their photographs became emblems of a period that embraced empowerment, individualism, and diversity.

Empowerment and Advocacy: Post-'90s, they have utilized their prominence to campaign for critical social problems, from maternal health to diversity and inclusion. Their joint activism has brought a beneficial change in society.

Enduring Friendship: Their enduring friendship and camaraderie have withstood the traditional rivalries of the industry. They praised each other's triumphs and supported one another during both personal and professional struggles.

The Supermodel Squad jointly demonstrated that models could be more than simply clothing hangers; they could be forces of change and champions for social causes. Their effect on the world of fashion, beauty, and culture serves as a testament to the strength of collective action and the enduring impact they've had on the industry and society.

6:1 Friendship and Camaraderie

The relationship and camaraderie among Linda Evangelista, Christy Turlington, Naomi Campbell, and Cindy Crawford is a strong and enduring bond that extends beyond the glamour and flash of the fashion industry. Their bonds have withstood the test of time and have survived the industry's competitiveness. A peek at their extraordinary friendships is provided here:

Solidarity in the Industry: Despite the intense competition that surrounded these supermodels when they first came to prominence, they opted to stand by one another. They honored each other's accomplishments and their friendship transcended the usual rivalries.

Mutual Respect: Christy Turlington, Linda Evangelista, Naomi Campbell, and Cindy Crawford respected one another's gifts and achievements. They understood that each contributed something unique to the realm of fashion.

Supportive Confidantes: They developed a close bond as confidantes, helping one another through both personal and professional victories in a field that frequently requires resiliency.

Enduring Friendships: Their bonds have lasted decades beyond the catwalk. The relationships they formed during their ascent to fame and the experiences they shared have endured.

Collaborations: As a result of their friendship, they have worked together on several fashion projects and well-known photo shoots, producing moments that will live on in the fashion business.

These Supermodel Queens not only helped to define a time, but they also demonstrated the strength of friendship and camaraderie. Their friendship highlights the value of encouraging one another as they work toward common goals and success and is proof of the strong relationships that can develop even in the most hostile settings.

6:2 Defining an Era Together

Together, Christy Turlington, Naomi Campbell, Cindy Crawford, and Linda Evangelista effectively ushered in a new chapter in fashion history. Beyond being supermodels, they embodied cultural icons whose impact extended beyond the catwalks and glossy fashion publications. Combined, they

Rekindled the Supermodel Phenomenon: The 1990s supermodel movement was greatly influenced by these four supermodels. They revolutionized the fashion business with their mesmerizing presence in fashion advertisements and on runways.

Championed Diversity: They stood out as trailblazers, dispelling preconceptions and advocating for a more inclusive definition of beauty during a time when diversity in the fashion industry was frequently absent.

Inspired Versatility: Their adaptability and capacity to assume several identities during a runway show demonstrated their dynamic variety, influencing fellow models, photographers, and designers.

Influential Trends in Fashion: They set fashion trends that are still relevant today; they were trendsetters. Their memorable fashion moments have had a lasting impression on the business.

Advanced Social Issues: Since the 1990s, they have made use of their notoriety to promote significant social issues, mainly those related to diversity, maternal health, and the welfare of children.

Became Cultural Icons: These supermodels went beyond the realm of fashion to become globally recognizable cultural icons who were often mentioned in movies, TV series, music videos, and popular culture.

Left an Enduring Legacy: Their legacy is a constant source of inspiration for the fashion industry and a reminder that genuine icons have a lasting impact on their era and beyond.

With their grace, beauty, adaptability, and advocacy, Christy Turlington, Naomi Campbell, Cindy Crawford, and Linda Evangelista characterized a period in fashion and society. These individuals represent empowerment, diversity, and long-lasting influence; they are more than just fashion icons. Collectively, they captured the essence of a time that expanded the roles available to supermodels and opened doors for a more diverse and exciting fashion industry.

CHAPTER 7: RUNWAY TO LEGACY: POST-90'S CAREERS

Known by many as the "Supermodel Queens," these iconic supermodels made a smooth transition from their 1990s runway careers to leave enduring legacies in a variety of disciplines. They continue to have a huge impact on the fashion industry, but they have also made important post-1990s careers for themselves. Let's examine their incredible travels:

1.Linda Evangelista: The Chameleon:
 - flexibility: Both on and off the runway, Linda Evangelista has been known for her flexibility. She has kept up her modeling career since the 1990s, working with esteemed companies and photographers to showcase her classic beauty.

Advocate for Maternal Health: Her support of maternal health and her founding of "Every Mother Counts" show her dedication to significant social problems.

2. Christy Turlington: Timeless Grace:

- Maternal Health Champion: Christy Turlington leaves a legacy through her commitment to advocating for maternal health. She started "Every Mother Counts" and has actively contributed to the advancement of maternity healthcare around the world.

- Documentary Filmmaker: Turlington has dabbled in the field of documentary filmmaking, producing powerful productions that highlight significant social and medical concerns.

3. Naomi Campbell: The Catwalk Queen:

- Fashion Icon: Naomi Campbell is still very much in the fashion world. She still graces covers, walks the runways, and collaborates with well-known designers, exhibiting her classic beauty and sense of style.

- Diversity and Inclusion Advocate: Her support of these causes has changed the fashion business to better reflect the diversity of the world.

4. Cindy Crawford: The Icon of America for All:
- Enterprises: After making the move from modeling to entrepreneurship, Cindy Crawford launched popular furniture collections and cosmetic product lines.

- Philanthropy: Her dedication to giving back is demonstrated by her enthusiastic support of children's hospitals and her participation in charitable endeavors that enhance the lives of children.

These four supermodels have shown that the '90s fashion scene is not the only place where their legacies can be found. They have changed over time, entered new industries, and are still significant in the twenty-first century. Their careers have carried them beyond the catwalk to the worlds of advocacy, business, filmmaking, and philanthropy; as a result, they are now considered true icons whose impact extends beyond the fashion industry.

7:1 Evolutions, Ventures, and Activism

Known as the "Supermodel Queens," these four legendary supermodels have not only changed with style but have also stepped into new areas and taken an active part in significant action. A closer look at their changes, business endeavors, and advocacy efforts is provided below:

1.Linda Evangelista: The Chameleon:

-Versatility:Linda Evangelista, who is renowned for her ability to change like a chameleon on the catwalk, has shown that flexibility and adaptability are necessary for long-term success in the fashion industry.

- Maternal Health Advocate: By turning her celebrity into an advocate, Evangelista has developed a strong stance in favor of maternal health. Her work has raised awareness of the vital issues surrounding maternal mortality and the significance of safe childbirth.

2. Christy Turlington: Timeless Grace:

-Simplicity and Elegance: Christy Turlington's hallmark has always been her timeless grace and elegance. Her enduring appeal is highlighted by her dedication to elegance and simplicity in both fashion and beauty.

- Maternal Health advocate: Turlington is now an advocate for maternal health, going above and beyond the runway. "Every Mother Counts," her organization, is a testament to her commitment to improving maternal healthcare across the globe and lowering avoidable maternal mortality.

3. Naomi Campbell: The Catwalk Queen:

-Striking Features and Timeless Beauty: Naomi Campbell's remarkable features and ageless beauty have helped her maintain her status as a significant figure in the fashion industry. She is still admired for her remarkable and distinctive features.

- Diversity and Inclusion Advocate: Campbell has gained prominence in the fashion business due to her support of diversity and inclusion. Her campaigning encourages better representation of models from diverse origins and challenges industry conventions.

4.Cindy Crawford: The All-American Icon:
-Natural Beauty: The timeless qualities of Cindy Crawford's appeal have been her unforced beauty and simplicity. Her dedication to maintaining a tidy appearance accentuates her classic elegance.

- Entrepreneurship: Crawford's forays into the commercial sector, such as her furniture collections and beauty product lines, demonstrate her aptitude for success. Her spirit of entrepreneurship has enabled her to expand her sphere of influence.

- Children's Welfare: Crawford is a strong advocate for charitable endeavors aimed at enhancing the lives of children, including children's hospitals. Her dedication to having a good influence outside of the fashion industry is demonstrated by her charitable endeavors.

These supermodels have demonstrated how their changes, endeavors, and activism have not only maintained their status but also allowed them to significantly affect causes that are close to their hearts. Their transitions from well-known fashionistas to powerful campaigners and businesspeople are evidence of their continuing significance and influence.

7-2 Leaving a Mark Beyond the Catwalk

These legendary supermodels have not only walked the most renowned runways in the world, but they have also had a lasting impression on a wide range of social issues, going well beyond the catwalk. A closer look at the significant contributions Linda Evangelista, Christy Turlington, Naomi Campbell, and Cindy Crawford have made outside of the fashion industry is provided here:

Leadership and Charity: These supermodels have made better use of their notoriety. They have devoted their lives to improving access to safe birthing and lowering maternal mortality as champions for maternal health. Their global awareness-raising and life-saving maternal health advocacy initiatives have made a significant impact.

Diversity and Inclusion: Naomi Campbell has been a steadfast supporter of these concepts in the fashion business. Her impact has been significant in questioning established conventions within the industry and advocating for increased representation of models with a range of racial, ethnic, and cultural origins.

Entrepreneurship: Cindy Crawford has successfully ventured into the world of business, introducing lines of furniture and cosmetic products. Her entrepreneurial endeavors have demonstrated her capacity to flourish in the business sector and broaden her impact across several industries.

Children's Welfare: Cindy Crawford has participated in charitable endeavors targeted at enhancing the lives of children and actively supports children's hospitals. Her commitment to enhancing the well-being of youngsters extends beyond the realm of fashion.

Cultural Icons: These supermodels are symbols of culture rather than just famous people in the fashion industry. Their pictures are well-known, and they frequently appear in TV shows and music videos, among other media, making a lasting impression on popular culture.

Persistent Style Influence: Their classic photos and fashion moments from the past still have an impact on modern culture. Their enduring influence on the fashion industry is demonstrated by the classic attractiveness of their style selections and their capacity to establish trends.

Cindy Crawford, Christy Turlington, Naomi Campbell, and Linda Evangelista have a profound impact that extends well beyond the glamorous world of modeling. Their commitment to diversity, entrepreneurship, philanthropy, activism, and children's welfare, in addition to their influence on culture and fashion, highlight their significant social impact. Supermodels such as these have demonstrated that real icons have an impact that goes well beyond the catwalk.

CHAPTER 8: THE IMPACT ON FASHION AND CULTURE

Together, Christy Turlington, Naomi Campbell, Cindy Crawford, and Linda Evangelista have made a lasting impression on the fashion and cultural industries. Their impact is felt far beyond the runway, permeating society conventions and the very fabric of elegance and beauty. A closer look at their influence on culture and fashion is provided here:

Redefining Beauty: As a group, these supermodels questioned accepted notions of beauty. They emphasized the value of accepting individuality by expanding the definition of beauty with their varied appearances.

Versatility and Adaptability: They were revolutionary in their ability to change and reinvent themselves, frequently in the course of a single photo session. It demonstrated their adaptability and mirrored the energy of the fashion sector.

Empowerment and Resilience: The inspirational tales of the Supermodel Queens are a source of strength and courage. Their stories of rising from humble origins to international renown serve as examples of how one may develop oneself and persevere in a very cut throat industry.

Culture Icons: These supermodels have attained the position of culture icons in addition to being fashion idols. Their well-known pictures frequently act as reminders of a time when glitz, uniqueness, and a feeling of empowerment were prized.

Influence and Trends in Fashion: The fashion industry is still influenced by its sense of style and the trends it establishes. They've shown how a distinct personality and sense of style can enhance fashion, opening the door for other models to become more than just clothing hangers.

Aspiring Models' Role Models: Aspiring models can find inspiration from their rise from obscurity to stardom. Their experiences show that success in the field may be attained by perseverance, commitment, and sincerity.

Timelessness: The fact that these Supermodel Queens are still honored and mentioned confirms their significance and attractiveness over time. Even now, their enduring fashion moments and pictures have a lasting impact.

It is impossible to overestimate the influence of Christy Turlington, Linda Evangelista, Naomi Campbell, and Cindy Crawford on fashion and culture. Their impact has not only influenced the fashion business but also redefined beauty standards, encouraged individualism, and motivated countless people to adopt their sense of style. The domains of fashion and culture are still feeling the effects of their enduring legacy.

8:1 Fashion, Beauty, and Pop Culture

In the fields of pop culture, fashion, and beauty, Linda Evangelista, Christy Turlington, Naomi Campbell, and Cindy Crawford have all left a lasting legacy. Their tremendous influence continues to define trends and aesthetics in various areas. A look at their influence in these areas is as follows:

Cloth:

1. Runway Pioneers: These supermodels played a key role in shaping the 1980s and 1990s fashion scene. Their eye-catching appearances, adaptability, and commanding presence on the catwalk redefined expectations in the business.

2. Famous Fashion Moments: They were highlighted in storied advertising campaigns, such as Cindy Crawford's collaboration with Pepsi and Naomi Campbell's

appearances in Versace ads. Fashion history is inscribed with these campaigns.

3. Trendsetters: They are known for setting trends in fashion, both on and off the runway. What is deemed stylish has been greatly affected by them, from Linda Evangelista's ability to embrace multiple personas to Christy Turlington's timeless and beautiful style.

Vintage:

1. Redefined Beauty Standards: With their varied appearances—from Linda Evangelista's chameleon-like flexibility to Naomi Campbell's striking features—these supermodels questioned accepted notions of beauty.

2. Timeless Beauty: Their timeless charm and well-mannered aging have demonstrated that beauty is not just a feature of youth. They still stand for timeless beauty.

3. Beauty Product Lines: Cindy Crawford, for example, has introduced her skincare brand and is opening it up to the public.

[Pop Culture]:

1. Cultural Icons: Cindy, Christy, Linda, and Naomi have transcended the realm of fashion to become symbols of culture. Their pictures have been well recognized and frequently appear in movies, TV series, and music videos.

2. Influence in Entertainment: They are well-known outside of the fashion industry thanks to their contributions to popular TV series, acting parts, and music videos.

3. Pop Culture References: From their signature poses to their catchphrases, these supermodels have left a lasting impression and are regularly mentioned in pop culture.

Beyond simply being supermodels, Linda Evangelista, Christy Turlington, Naomi Campbell, and Cindy Crawford are icons of grace, elegance, and enduring power in the fields of pop culture, fashion, and beauty. Generation after generation of viewers are enthralled and inspired by their legacies.

8:2 The Enduring Legacy of the Supermodel Queens

The legacies of Linda Evangelista, Christy Turlington, Naomi Campbell, and Cindy Crawford shine brightly in the ever-evolving world of fashion and beauty, leaving an enduring and unforgettable mark on the business they have adorned for decades. Known as the "Supermodel Queens," these four legendary supermodels have left a lasting impact that cuts beyond fashion and time.

Their influence on pop culture, beauty, and fashion is immense. A sample of the lasting legacy they have created is as follows:

Defining Beauty Standards: By questioning accepted notions of beauty, the Supermodel Queens have demonstrated that diversity can be beautiful. Their presence has expanded the meaning of beauty and highlighted the value of individuality.

Adaptation and Versatility: These supermodels, who are well-known for their versatility and adaptation, have shown that change is not only inevitable but also something to be welcomed. Their timeless appeal is demonstrated by their capacity to change with the times and remain relevant.

Empowerment and Resilience: Throughout their careers, the Supermodel Queens have overcome adversity and come out stronger and with greater resilience. Their inspiring tales of tenacity and resolve serve as an example to everybody.

Philanthropy and Advocacy: These enduring supermodels have championed important causes, like as diversity in the fashion business and maternal health, by using their notoriety. They have changed the world for the better by using their influence.

Cultural Icons: They have transcended the runway to become icons of culture, evoking a period and shaping social norms. People of all ages are still moved and inspired by their pictures and stories.

Influence and Trends in Fashion: The Supermodel Queens have influenced a great deal of fashion and are still an inspiration to both designers and fashionistas. The fashion industry continues to draw inspiration from their wardrobe selections.

Aspiring Models' Role Models: Aspiring models might find hope in their enduring legacy, which demonstrates that success can be attained with perseverance, hard effort, and uniqueness.

Timelessness: Their continuing impact confirms that they are timeless. Their classic looks and fashion moments from the past are still relevant and referenced in modern fashion.

These Supermodel Queens have written a part of fashion and beauty history that will never go away. Their legacy serves as a reminder that genuine icons have a lasting impact on society and that future generations will be inspired by and shaped by their influence in the entertainment industry. With their eternal legacy, the Supermodel Queens continue to rule as the ultimate representations of resilience, empowerment, and beauty.

CHAPTER 9: BEYOND BEAUTY: PHILANTHROPY AND ADVOCACY

Through philanthropy and campaigning, the supermodel quartet of Linda Evangelista, Christy Turlington, Naomi Campbell, and Cindy Crawford goes beyond their glitzy occupations to significantly impact society. In addition to their breathtaking beauty and memorable fashion moments, these women have committed their lives to worthwhile causes. A closer look at their advocacy and philanthropic work is provided below:

Linda Evangelista:
 - Activist for Maternal Health: Maternal health is something Linda Evangelista supports. She uses her notoriety to draw attention to the global statistics of maternal death. Her work with "Every Mother Counts"

highlights how crucial it is for women all around the world to have access to safe childbirth.

Christy Turlington:

- Champion of Maternal Health: Christy Turlington is well known for her dedication to advocating for maternal health. She started "Every Mother Counts" to decrease needless maternal deaths and increase access to healthcare for mothers.

Naomi Campbell:

- Promoter of Diversity and Inclusion: Naomi Campbell is a strong proponent of inclusion and diversity in the fashion sector. She campaigns against systematic prejudices and for increased representation of models from a variety of racial and ethnic backgrounds by using her powerful voice.

Cindy Crawford:

- Philanthropist and Entrepreneur: Cindy Crawford has used her notoriety to further charitable causes. She participates in numerous charitable endeavors targeted at enhancing the lives of children and actively supports children's hospitals. Her influence has also gone beyond modeling because of her prosperous business endeavors.

These supermodels have demonstrated that beauty can be a positive influence in addition to gracing the most famous runways in the world. Their dedication to utilizing their celebrity to make a positive difference in the world is demonstrated by their advocacy and charitable endeavors. Above all, they are beautiful examples of the idea that genuine beauty comes from kindness, generosity, and a commitment to improving the world.

9:1 Using Fame for a Purpose

The great supermodels of their day, Linda Evangelista, Christy Turlington, Naomi Campbell, and Cindy Crawford, have used their notoriety to change society in significant ways. They have utilized their platforms for more than simply walking the most famous runways in the world. Here is how they have used their notoriety to further important causes:

Linda Evangelista:

- Activist for Maternal Health: Maternal health is something Linda Evangelista is passionate about promoting. Her involvement with "Every Mother Counts" has raised awareness of the vital problem of maternal mortality on a global scale.

Christy Turlington:

-Champion of Maternal Health: Also a well-known proponent of maternal health, Christy Turlington founded the organization "Every Mother Counts." She has brought attention to the significance of safe childbirth and the availability of high-quality healthcare.

Naomi Campbell:

- Promoter of Diversity and Inclusion: In the fashion industry, Naomi Campbell has been a strong voice for inclusion and diversity. Her voice has been crucial in breaking down barriers related to gender and race and advocating for increased representation.

Cindy Crawford:

- Philanthropist and Entrepreneur: Cindy Crawford has dabbled in business, introducing popular furniture collections and lines of cosmetic products. She also actively supports charitable initiatives aimed at enhancing the lives of children as well as children's hospitals.

These well-known supermodels have supported causes close to their hearts by using their resources, influence, and notoriety. Their dedication to improving society shows that celebrity can be a potent weapon for promoting change and building a better society. They are more than just style icons; they are role models who have profoundly impacted countless lives.

9.2 Contributions to Society and Causes

These four enduring supermodels have significantly impacted society and causes by leveraging their notoriety and influence to raise awareness of crucial concerns and have a beneficial effect in several ways:

1. Linda Evangelista:

 - Maternal Health Advocacy: Linda Evangelista is the creator of the "Every Mother Counts" initiative and a champion for maternal health. She strives to increase global access to safe birthing and increase awareness of maternal mortality.

2. Christy Turlington:

- Advocacy for Maternal Health: A well-known proponent of maternal health, Christy Turlington founded the organization "Every Mother Counts." She has committed her work to raising maternal health, lowering avoidable birth-related deaths, and giving moms everywhere access to care.

3. Naomi Campbell:

-Diversity and Inclusion: Naomi Campbell has made a strong case for these concepts in the fashion business. She has pushed for increased representation of models from varied backgrounds and challenged industry conventions using her platform.

 - Humanitarian Work: Campbell has contributed to numerous philanthropic projects and has collaborated with groups such as the White Ribbon Alliance.

4. Cindy Crawford:

 - Entrepreneurship: Cindy Crawford entered the furniture and beauty product industries and launched profitable lines of products. Her business endeavors demonstrate her aptitude for success in the business sector.

- Advocacy for Youth: Crawford has actively participated in charitable endeavors aimed at enhancing the lives of children and has supported children's hospitals.

Supermodels like these have demonstrated that their impact goes well beyond the catwalk and fashion magazine pages. Using their wealth and notoriety, they have contributed significantly to issues close to their hearts, ranging from diversity in the fashion business and maternal health to the welfare of children and entrepreneurship. Their philanthropy and advocacy endeavors serve as evidence of their dedication to bringing about constructive social change.

CHAPTER 10: THE QUEENS' SECRETS: BEAUTY, FASHION, AND WELLNESS

Over the years, these enduring supermodels—dubbed the "Queens" of the fashion industry—have not only preserved their attractiveness and sense of style, but they have also divulged their beauty, wellness, and fashion secrets. Here's an overview of their perspectives and methods:

Linda Evangelista: The Chameleon:
- Beauty Secrets: Linda Evangelista's healthy lifestyle and skincare regimen are credited for her enduring beauty. She stresses how crucial it is to properly cleanse, moisturize, and protect yourself from the sun.

- Fashion Wisdom: Linda Evangelista, who is renowned for her adaptability, offers fashion advice that revolves around trying out many looks and being willing to adapt. She exhorts people to embrace their individuality in style preferences.

- Wellness Tip: Linda Evangelista incorporates exercise, a nutritious diet, and stress reduction into her daily routine as part of a balanced approach to wellness. She thinks that a person's outward represents their inner well-being.

Christy Turlington: Classic Beauty:
Beauty Secrets: Christy Turlington keeps her beauty routine simple. She stays hydrated and uses clean, natural skincare products to keep her complexion looking glowing, and she favors natural makeup.

- Fashion Wisdom: Christy Turlington has a timeless, refined style. She values making investments in classic pieces that will last for many years and stresses the significance of sustainability in the fashion industry.

- Wellness Tip: For mental and physical health, Turlington engages in yoga and meditation. Her work for maternal health is a testament to her commitment to wellness.

Naomi Campbell: The Queen of the Catwalk:
- Beauty Secrets: Naomi Campbell's remarkable features are well-known. A strict skincare regimen, frequent facials, and adequate hydration are some of her secrets to beauty. When not on the job, she supports keeping one's face fresh and makeup-free.

- Fashion Wisdom: Campbell's audacious and self-assured aesthetic is a reflection of who she is. She exhorts people to be bold with their wardrobe choices and to embrace their individuality.

- Wellness Tip: Naomi Campbell places a high value on mental and self-care. Despite her hectic schedule, she maintains her composure and sense of center by doing yoga and meditation.

Cindy Crawford: The Icon of All America:

-Beauty Secrets: Cindy Crawford keeps her skin looking radiant by following a regular skincare routine and emphasizing water intake. She is an advocate of embracing one's inherent attractiveness.

- Fashion Wisdom: Crawford has a traditional yet laid-back aesthetic. She emphasizes the importance of confidence in both appearance and well-being while advocating for casual yet stylish clothing.

- Wellness Tip: Cindy Crawford encourages regular exercise, a healthy diet, and an optimistic mindset to enhance general well-being. She highlights the holistic nature of the pursuit of wellness.

These supermodel queens value wellness as a vital aspect of their lives in addition to being the epitome of classic beauty and style. Many people find inspiration in their beauty, fashion, and wellness recommendations, which is a testament to their continuing appeal and influence on the beauty and fashion industries.

10:1 Beauty and Fashion Insights

Over the years, legendary supermodels Linda Evangelista, Christy Turlington, Naomi Campbell, and Cindy Crawford have given priceless beauty and fashion ideas. They are well-known individuals in the fashion and cosmetics industry thanks to their classic looks and enduring beauty. Their main discoveries are as follows:

Linda Evangelista: The Chameleon:

- Versatility: Linda Evangelista's ability to change and adapt to different styles is praised for being similar to that of a chameleon. She advocates trying out various outfits and embracing adaptability.

- Classic Beauty: She stresses the value of a simple, classic beauty regimen that includes good skincare and little cosmetics for a youthful, timeless appearance.

- Confidence: Evangelista's success has been largely attributed to her self-assurance and confidence on the catwalk and in front of the camera. She promotes confidence in oneself as a crucial component of one's style.

Christy Turlington: Classic Beauty:
- Natural Beauty: Christy Turlington's graceful and natural beauty hasn't changed over time. She promotes natural cosmetics and uncluttered skincare as key components of straightforward beauty regimens.

- Timeless Style: Timeless elegance and minimalism define Turlington's style. She thinks that investing in timeless, high-quality items is wise.

- wellbeing: She places a great value on wellbeing and emphasizes the need to lead a balanced lifestyle by engaging in yoga and meditation for both mental and physical health.

Naomi Campbell: The Queen of the Catwalk:
- Striking Features: Naomi Campbell is a legendary figure thanks to her striking features. She emphasizes

how regular facials, hydration, and maintenance are essential to maintaining her glowing skin.

- Fearless Fashion: Campbell has set trends in the fashion industry thanks to her audacious and fearless sense of style. She exhorts people to own their individuality and have confidence in their wardrobe selections.

- Wellness and Balance: To keep her mental health and equilibrium in her hectic life, Naomi does yoga and meditation. She puts herself first.

Cindy Crawford: The Icon of All America:
-Natural attractiveness: One of Cindy Crawford's most well-known qualities is her inherent attractiveness. She stresses the need to maintain one's natural self and keep beauty regimens simple.

Confidence and Comfort: Crawford has a classic yet laid-back sense of style. She exhorts individuals to strike a balance between dressing stylishly and comfortably.

- *Overall Wellness: Cindy places a strong emphasis on maintaining general health through consistent exercise, a healthy diet, and an optimistic outlook. Her understanding of wellbeing well-being is pensive.

These supermodel role models have taught us important lessons about accepting simplicity, adaptability, and self-assurance in terms of appearance and style. Their classic elegance and enduring beauty continue to serve as an inspiration to a great number of people and demonstrate their enormous impact on the fashion and beauty industries.

10:2 Staying Ageless and Stylish

These enduring supermodels continue to radiate ageless beauty and style, defying the expectations of the traditional age. Here are a few of their tips for being fashionable and timeless:

Versatility: Linda Evangelista, also known as "The Chameleon," has managed to maintain her relevance in the fashion industry through her ability to adapt and change with the times. She displays her dynamic style by embracing new trends and experimenting with various styles.

- Skincare Routine: To keep her perfect complexion, Evangelista adheres to a strict skincare regimen that emphasizes the value of adequate washing, moisturizing, and sun protection.

Christy Turlington's timeless grace is characterized by her simplicity, which also happens to be a defining feature of her beauty and style. She chooses simple, minimalist clothing and natural makeup so that her elegant, ageless beauty may be fully appreciated.

- Yoga and Wellness: For her physical and emotional health, Turlington engages in yoga and meditation. Her ageless beauty is a result of her commitment to holistic wellness.

Naomi Campbell: The Catwalk Queen

- Skincare Regimen: Naomi Campbell follows a strict skincare routine that emphasizes frequent facials and hydration. She emphasizes the value of healthy, beautiful skin by attributing her dazzling skin to these habits.

- Confident Fashion Choices: Campbell's daring and unafraid attitude to style is still a defining characteristic. She shows that keeping trendy requires confidence in being herself.

The All-American Icon: Cindy Crawford

- Natural Beauty: Cindy Crawford keeps up her natural beauty with an easy-to-follow beauty regimen. She promotes the use of high-quality, natural skincare products and minimum makeup.

- Timeless Style: Crawford's wardrobe combines comfort and classic elements. She thinks that investing in classic, cozy clothing will give her a polished, self-assured look.

These supermodels, who embrace simplicity, adaptability, and self-assurance, never cease to inspire with their timeless beauty and sense of style. Their focus on skincare, fashion, and wellness is a reflection of their ongoing appeal and significant influence on the beauty and fashion industries.

CONCLUSION

The enduring power of renowned supermodels is demonstrated by the legacies of Christy Turlington, Naomi Campbell, Cindy Crawford, Linda Evangelista, and Naomi Campbell in the domains of pop culture, fashion, and beauty. As we come to the end of our investigation into "The Queens of Fashion," we are reminded of the enormous influence these remarkable ladies have had on both the industry and society in general.

Beyond just having gorgeous faces, these supermodels are trailblazers who broke down barriers, rewrote the definition of beauty, and made a lasting impression on the fashion industry. Their chameleon-like adaptability, timelessness, and agility in a field that is constantly evolving have made them the real catwalk queens.

Their impact can be seen in the fields of wellness and beauty in addition to the runway. Their focus on wellness practices, simple skincare regimens, and simplicity emphasizes that everyone may achieve ageless beauty, which originates from within.

However, their contributions go above and beyond. These queens have made good use of their notoriety by supporting charitable organizations, diversity, inclusivity, and social causes. They have fought for social justice, supported women's rights, and increased public awareness of maternal health by utilizing their platforms.

Their fashion sense has imparted to us valuable lessons about adaptability, welcoming change, and discovering comfort and self-assurance in our styles. Numerous people have been motivated to stay true to themselves and to discover their sense of style by their ageless grace and style.

As this chapter comes to an end, the legacy of Christy Turlington, Linda Evangelista, Naomi Campbell, and Cindy Crawford endures and inspires those who want to defy expectations, celebrate diversity, and make a lasting impression on the world. They are more than just style icons; they are real queens, and future generations will honor their reign. Their impact serves as a constant reminder that certain queens rule supreme in the domains of pop culture, fashion, and beauty, and that their legacies are genuinely everlasting.

www.ingramcontent.com/pod-product-compliance
Lightning Source LLC
Chambersburg PA
CBHW062341290526
45794CB00005B/2071